Florence Nightingale

by
Shannon Zemlicka

illustrations by
Nicolas Debon

Carolrhoda Books, Inc./Minneapolis

The photograph on page 46 appears courtesy of © Bettmann/CORBIS

This book is available in two editions:
Library binding by Carolrhoda Books, Inc., a division of Lerner Publishing Group
Soft cover by First Avenue Editions, an imprint of Lerner Publishing Group
241 First Avenue North
Minneapolis, MN 55401 U.S.A.

Website address: www.lernerbooks.com

Library of Congress Cataloging-in-Publication Data

Zemlicka, Shannon.
    Florence Nightingale / by Shannon Zemlicka ; illustrations by Nicolas Debon.
       p.   cm. — (On my own biography)
    Summary: Introduces the life of Florence Nightingale, a pioneer of women's
nursing, including her childhood, training, work in the Crimean War, and her school
for nurses.
    Includes bibliographical references.
    ISBN: 0–87614–917–4 (lib. bdg. : alk. paper)
    ISBN: 0-87614-102-5 (pbk: alk. paper)
1. Nightingale, Florence, 1820–1910—Juvenile literature. 2. Nurses—England—
Biography—Juvenile literature. [1. Nightingale, Florence, 1820–1910. 2. Nurses.
3. Women—Biography.] I. Debon, Nicolas, ill. II. Title. III. Series.
    RT37.N5 Z464 2003
    610.73'092—dc21   2002000984

Manufactured in the United States of America
1 2 3 4 5 6 – JR – 08 07 06 05 04 03

For my mom, Brenda Barefield, who has always supported me in chasing my dreams — S.Z.

To François, Mathilde, and Tosca — N.D.

An Unusual Girl
England, 1826

Flo tied a sling around a doll's arm.

The poor girl had fallen.

Another doll needed a bandage.

It was a busy day for Flo.

All 18 of her dolls needed nursing.

She had to help them get well.

Most girls in England did not have
so many dolls.
But six-year-old Florence Nightingale
was not like most girls.
Her family was rich.

The Nightingales owned two huge houses
and lots of land.
They had servants to do their work
for them.
Flo and her sister, Parthe,
had ponies and fancy dresses.
They had all the dolls and toys
they could want.
As Flo grew older, she learned that most
people did not live as the Nightingales did.
Most people worked hard.
They lived in small, crowded houses.
Sometimes Flo's mother took her to visit
poor people who lived nearby.
But most of the time,
the Nightingales enjoyed themselves.

They went to parties and concerts.

They wrote letters and read books.

They were all happy—all except Flo.

She wanted to do more than enjoy herself.

She wanted to help people.

Flo began to worry about the suffering
she saw around her.
The poor people that she visited
were often sick.
Then, when she was nine,
illness struck her own family.
Her cousin Bonny became so sick
that his doctors couldn't help him.

Bonny tried to be brave,

but he hurt terribly.

Finally, he died.

There was so much sickness and pain

in the world, Flo thought.

What could she do to help?

Flo knew that her parents did not expect

her to spend her life helping people.

They expected her to do what

her mother had done.

When she grew up, she should marry

a rich man and raise a family.

She should live in a huge house

and have fun.

Flo loved her family very much.

But she hated the idea of a lifetime

of enjoying herself.

Too many people were suffering.

One day when Flo was 16,
something odd happened.
She was sitting under two cedar trees
at her family's winter home.
This quiet spot was one of her favorite
places to be alone.
Suddenly, she realized that she
wasn't alone at all.
A strange voice was speaking to her.
It asked her to serve.
Flo was sure that she had heard
the voice of God.
She didn't know what God
meant for her to do.
But she did know one thing.
She could not stand to live the way
her parents wanted her to.

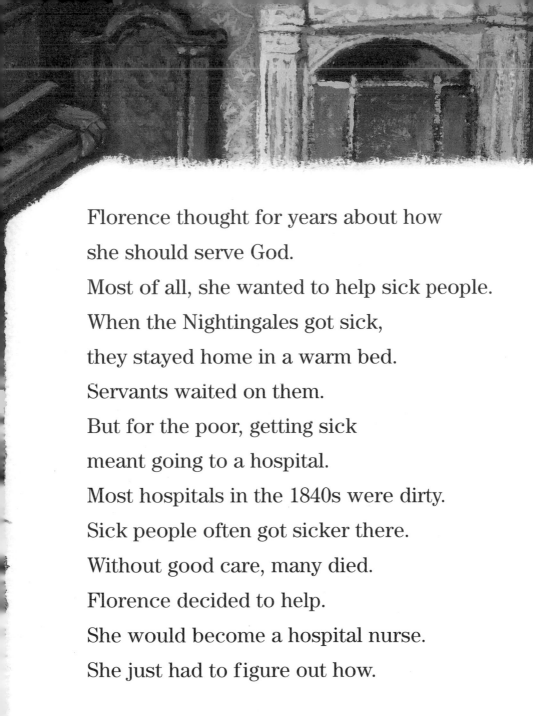

Florence thought for years about how
she should serve God.
Most of all, she wanted to help sick people.
When the Nightingales got sick,
they stayed home in a warm bed.
Servants waited on them.
But for the poor, getting sick
meant going to a hospital.
Most hospitals in the 1840s were dirty.
Sick people often got sicker there.
Without good care, many died.
Florence decided to help.
She would become a hospital nurse.
She just had to figure out how.

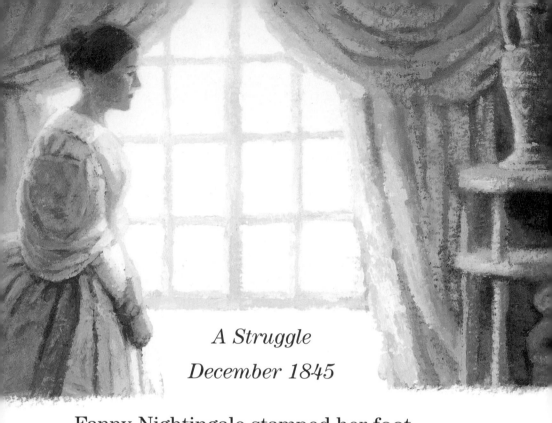

Fanny Nightingale stamped her foot.

Parthe flung herself onto a sofa

and began to sob.

Florence had told her mother and sister

that she wanted to study nursing.

They would not stand for it!

Florence must have lost her mind

to suggest such a thing.

Hospitals were terrible places,
Fanny reminded Florence.
Nurses were not ladies.
Many of them drank alcohol.
Even worse, they had to wash their
patients and change their clothes.
And many of those patients were men!

Florence's father was shocked, too.
He had raised his daughter to be
charming and smart.
He had raised her to find a good husband.
How could she be so ungrateful?

Florence was sadder

than she had ever been.

She could never disobey her family.

It would not be right.

Still, she did not give up.

She began to read about hospitals.

To keep her work secret,

she read before the sun came up.

Almost five years passed.
Florence was 29 years old
and more miserable than ever.
Then she went on a trip with two friends.
In Germany, she visited a nursing school.

At Kaiserswerth, dozens of women
were learning to care for the sick.
They seemed like perfect ladies to Florence.
Meeting them made her remember
her hopes for a useful life.

Back at home, Florence made a hard choice.

It was wrong to disobey her family.

But it was even worse to give up her life

just to please them.

She decided to go back to Kaiserswerth.

Fanny and Parthe raged at the news.

But Florence did not change her mind.

She trained for three months in 1851.

She learned to bandage wounds

and comfort people in pain.

Later, back in England, she found a job

running a hospital for women.

She began her new work in 1853.

She was helping the sick at last!

Florence loved caring for the women

at the hospital.

But soon she wondered about the future.

Could she do more to help people?

In August of 1854, Florence found the
answer to her question.

England had gone to war against Russia.

Thousands of soldiers had been wounded.

Many others had gotten sick.

The army needed people to care for them.

Florence's friend Sidney Herbert worked
for the government.

He wrote to her for help.

Would she lead a group of nurses?

The work would be very hard.

She would be far from home,
in a country called Turkey.

Florence knew that she was meant
to do this job.

She hired nurses and packed her bags.

She was on her way to work at war.

War Nurse

Scutari, Turkey

November 5, 1854

Florence could hardly believe her eyes.
She had known that the Barrack Hospital
needed nurses.
But she had not expected what she saw now.

The hospital had no beds.

Wounded men lay on the floor.

There were no clean blankets
to keep the men warm.

There were no clean bandages
to cover their wounds.

There was hardly even any medicine.

Then Florence heard more bad news.
The doctors did not want her help!
The army had never had women nurses.
The doctors did not want a rich lady
telling them how to heal people.
Florence and her nurses could hear
the wounded men crying out in pain.
But they could not help.
They sewed shirts and made
bandages instead.

Everything changed on November 9.

Ship after ship came to Scutari.

Each was filled with sick and
wounded men.

The doctors had no time to worry
about women nurses now.

Every hand was needed.

Florence and the nurses went to work.

They washed the men
and bandaged their wounds.

They stuffed sacks with straw
to make beds.

At night, Florence did not rest.

She walked among the beds,
carrying a lamp.

She comforted the men
as well as she could.

When Florence was not nursing,
she asked questions.
She began to see why the hospital
was such a terrible place.
The army had money to buy supplies.
But no one could agree
who should buy them.

If the wrong officer spent money,
he got in trouble.
Florence had her own money to spend.
She wasn't afraid of trouble.
So she bought supplies herself.
She bought shirts and socks,
forks and knives, towels and soap.

Florence solved other problems, too.

No one was cleaning the floors and walls.

Blood and dirt covered them like slime.

Florence bought brushes for scrubbing.

The nurses cleaned the hospital themselves.

No one was washing the soldiers' clothes.

Florence paid soldiers' wives

to do the work.

Slowly, the Barrack Hospital
became less miserable.
The soldiers knew who to thank—
Florence Nightingale.
They kissed her shadow as she
walked past their beds.

As Florence got things done,

the doctors began to trust her.

But not everyone liked her.

The army officers who ran the hospital

were embarrassed by her.

Her work showed how poorly

they had done their jobs.

Some of the nurses did not like her, either.

She was kind to the soldiers,

but very strict with the nurses.

She cared much more about her work

than about what others thought of her.

In May of 1855, Florence went to visit

other army hospitals.

She found them dirty and badly run.

Florence had many ideas.

She could make these hospitals better,

just as she had done at Scutari.

But before she could begin,
she got sick with a fever.
She almost died.

Florence went back to Scutari.

She had to rest for weeks.

But she would not go home to England.

There was too much work to be done.

Florence kept on solving problems.

When soldiers began to get well,

they had nothing useful to do.

Most went to bars and drank alcohol.

Drinking often made them sick

all over again.

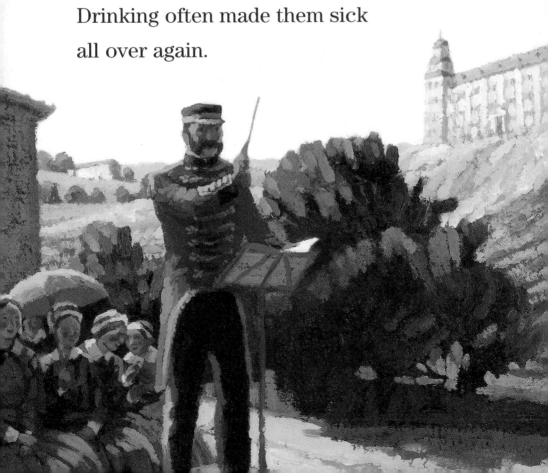

Florence helped find teachers
to start schools for the soldiers.
Instead of drinking,
the men went to classes.
They learned to sing.
They put on plays
and held soccer matches.

In 1856, England made peace with Russia.

The Crimean War ended.

As the last men at Scutari got well,

they went home.

By July, they were all gone.

Florence went home, too.

She had proved that women

made good war nurses.

She had helped thousands of soldiers.

Yet she felt like a failure.

She could think only about the thousands

who had died in the army's hospitals.

Would people keep dying

in unhealthy hospitals?

What could she do to make a difference?

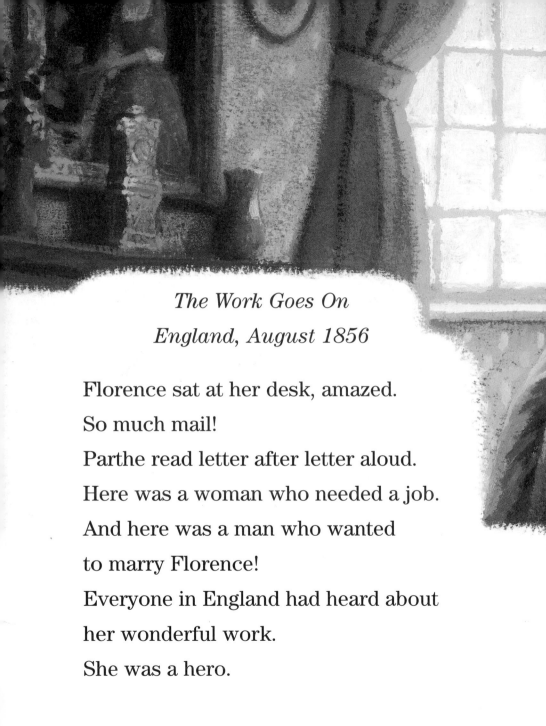

The Work Goes On
England, August 1856

Florence sat at her desk, amazed.

So much mail!

Parthe read letter after letter aloud.

Here was a woman who needed a job.

And here was a man who wanted
to marry Florence!

Everyone in England had heard about
her wonderful work.

She was a hero.

Florence did not want to be a hero.

She did not want to get married.

She only wanted to keep helping soldiers.

The long months at Scutari
had left her very ill.
Often she could not leave her room.
But she could still work
to make hospitals better.
She wrote letters and reports to
the government to explain her ideas.
She held meetings.
Sometimes she worked 22 hours a day.
Florence also opened a school
for nurses in 1860.
The students lived together at
a hospital in London.
Florence was too sick to train them herself.
But she wrote to them and visited them.
She was proud to see her school's nurses
sent to hospitals all over the world.

Years went by, and still Florence worked.

Thanks to her efforts,

health care improved in the army

and in the British colony of India.

In 1893, Florence turned 73.

She began to rest at last.

Of course, she still worked sometimes.

But she could look back on her life

and see how much good she had done.

As a girl, she had felt it was wrong
to have too much fun.
Now she read books and had visitors.
She played with her pet cats.
After all her years of work,
Florence Nightingale could finally
enjoy herself.

Afterword

Florence died in 1910 at the age of 90. She left behind safer, cleaner hospitals where trained nurses played an important role in caring for patients. Hospitals in many countries adopted her ideas. Many lives were saved as a result.

Florence helped create an important change for women, too. When she began her work, women had few ways to earn money. Those who became nurses often faced the scorn and shame that the Nightingales felt. After her success in the Crimean War, more people began to see nursing as an honorable profession. When Florence opened her school, she created a new path for English women who shared her dream.

It would have been easy for Florence Nightingale to live a life of comfort. Instead, she lived as she believed she should, working hard to help others. Her determination to be useful became an example for the entire world.

Important Dates

1820—Florence Nightingale was born in Florence, Italy, on May 12.

1821—Returned to England with family

1837—Heard what she believed to be the voice of God calling her to serve

1845—Request to study nursing rejected by family

1850—Visited Kaiserswerth in Germany

1851—Returned to Kaiserswerth for training

1853—Began first job, running a women's hospital

1854—Led group of nurses to Scutari, Turkey, to nurse soldiers in Crimean War

1856—Returned to England; began working to improve hospitals

1860—Opened Nightingale Training School for nurses in London

1910—Died on August 13 in London, England